NFL RIVALRIES

STEELERS VS. RAVENS

By Karen Price

Kaleidoscope
Minneapolis, MN

Your Front Row Seat to the Games

This edition first published in 2020 by Kaleidoscope Publishing, Inc.

For information regarding permission, write to
Kaleidoscope Publishing, Inc.
6012 Blue Circle Drive
Minnetonka, MN 55343

Library of Congress Control Number
2019939220

ISBN
978-1-64519-084-4 (library bound)
978-1-64494-169-0 (paperback)
978-1-64519-185-8 (ebook)

Printed in the United States of America.

TABLE OF CONTENTS

CHAPTER 1

Battle for the Bowl

The noise was deafening. Fans at Pittsburgh's Heinz Field were yelling. The Baltimore Ravens players could barely hear. That helped the home team. The Pittsburgh Steelers defenders got into position. Ravens **rookie** quarterback Joe Flacco then took the **snap**. A huge play was underway.

This was a big game. The rivals were two of the best teams in the National Football League (NFL) in 2008. Now they met in the playoffs. The winner would go to the Super Bowl.

Less than five minutes remained in the game. The Ravens trailed 16–14. This was their chance. Flacco looked around the field. Then he saw his man. The quarterback threw the ball to the right. It never made it to its target.

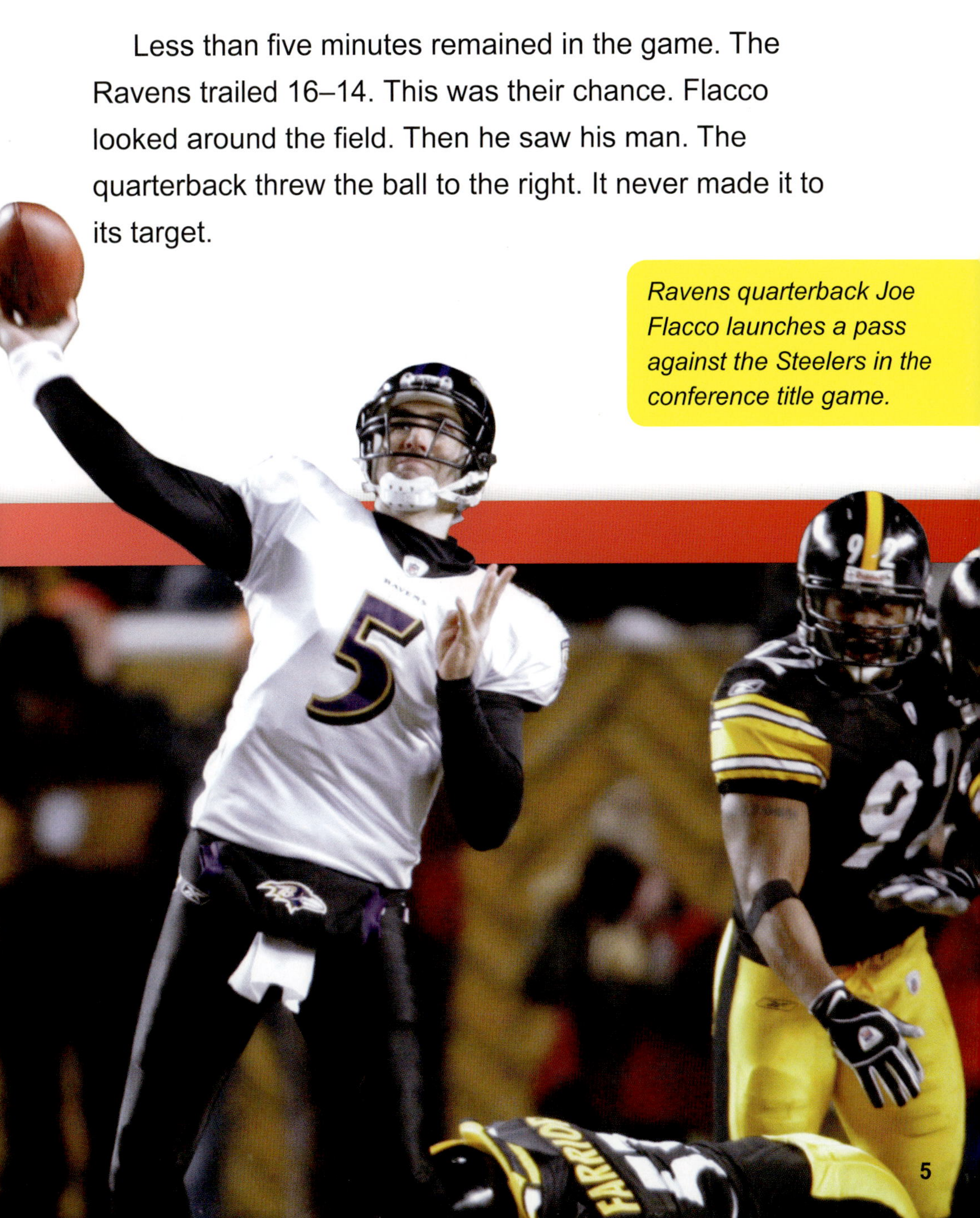

Ravens quarterback Joe Flacco launches a pass against the Steelers in the conference title game.

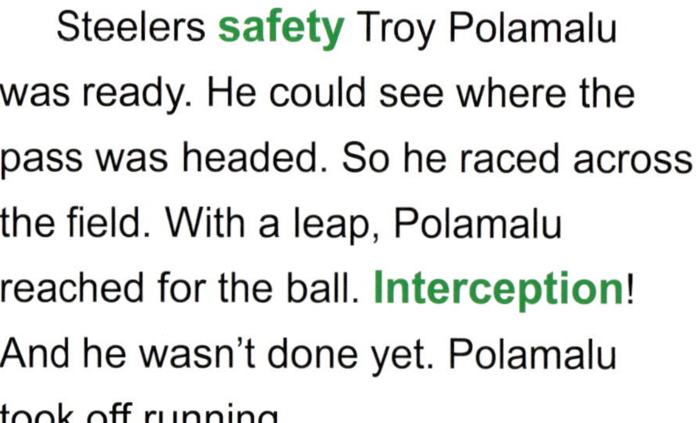

Steelers **safety** Troy Polamalu was ready. He could see where the pass was headed. So he raced across the field. With a leap, Polamalu reached for the ball. **Interception**! And he wasn't done yet. Polamalu took off running.

He zig-zagged across the field. He dodged to his right. Then he ran all the way to the other side. Polamalu wanted to score. He ran into the end zone and pointed up at the Steelers fans. Everyone jumped to their feet. Fans cheered. Some waved their yellow towels. Others gave each other high-fives.

FUN FACT

The Ravens are one of two NFL teams to have their own marching band.

Troy Polamalu runs away from Ravens players on his way to the end zone.

The Steelers and the Ravens were already fierce rivals. Every game they played was tough. Both teams wanted to win. But this game was special.

Flacco was coming off a great year. No rookie quarterback had ever led his team to the Super Bowl. The Ravens thought he could be the first. But to do so they had to get through Pittsburgh. The Steelers had the best defense in the NFL. Polamalu proved that. His interception sealed the game. The Steelers pulled ahead 23–14. That's how the game ended. And two weeks later, the Steelers won their sixth Super Bowl.

With the win over the Ravens, Polamalu and the Steelers were headed to the Super Bowl.

TROY POLAMALU'S INTERCEPTION

Ravens quarterback Joe Flacco took the snap at his own 29-yard line. He passed to the right. It was intended for receiver Derrick Mason. Instead, Steelers safety Troy Polamalu jumped in the air and caught it for an interception at the 40-yard line. He then ran all the way across the field for a touchdown. It helped clinch a 23–14 Steelers win.

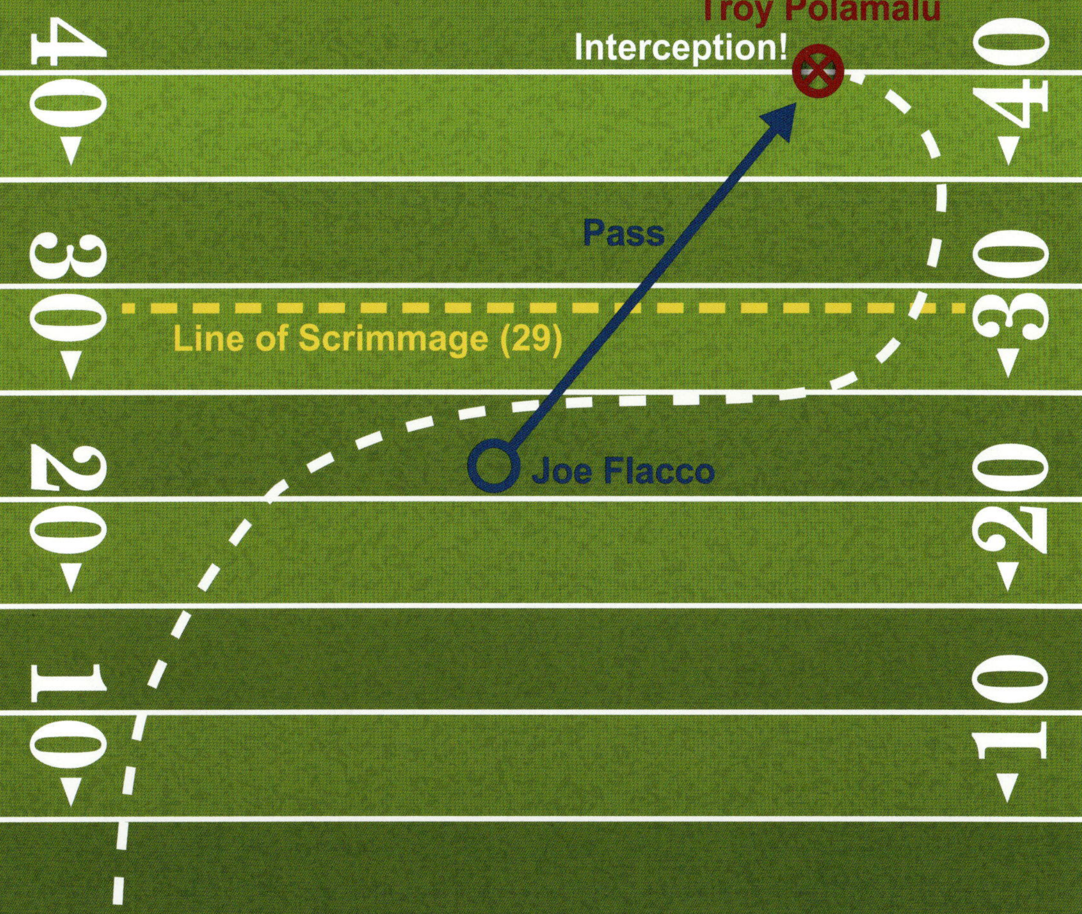

CHAPTER 2

Old Is New Again

A slight wind blew through Three Rivers Stadium. It was September 8, 1996. The season was only one week old. Yet the Pittsburgh Steelers were already 0–1. They needed a win. The Baltimore Ravens had other ideas.

The Ravens were in their first season. They weren't brand new, though. They had been the Cleveland Browns. The Browns and Steelers were rivals. Then the Browns moved to Baltimore. They became the Ravens.

Rod Woodson was ready. The Steelers cornerback intercepted a pass. Then he returned it for a touchdown. That helped boost Pittsburgh to a 31–17 win. The new rivalry was just getting started.

SUPER STANDOUTS

The Ravens began play in 1996. Four years later, they won a Super Bowl. The 2012 Ravens won another championship. Pittsburgh has won six Super Bowls. That is tied for the most. Two came after 1996. The Steelers won it all in the 2005 and 2008 seasons.

Pittsburgh's Jerome Bettis bulldozes his way into the end zone in the team's first game against the Ravens.

The 2010 Steelers won the **division**. Baltimore finished second. On January 15, 2011, they met in a playoff game. The Steelers scored first. But Baltimore then came back. By halftime, the Ravens led by fourteen.

The Steelers weren't giving up. They tied the game 24–24. Two minutes remained. Pittsburgh had the ball again. But it was third down. The Steelers had 19 yards to go. Quarterback Ben Roethlisberger took the snap. He dropped back. Then he launched the ball in the air. It soared 58 yards downfield. Rookie Antonio Brown made the catch. The ball stuck to his hands like glue. The Steelers scored five plays later. That secured a 31–24 win.

COMPLICATED RIVALRIES

The Steelers and Browns first met in 1950. They became rivals. Then in 1996 the Browns left for Baltimore. The Steelers and Ravens became rivals. But a new Browns team started in 1999. The old rivalry resumed. Baltimore and Pittsburgh were no strangers, either. The Colts played in Baltimore from 1953–1983. They met the Steelers twice in the playoffs. But Pittsburgh won both.

Rivalry Map
N
W
E
S
Maine
Vermont
New Hampshire
New York
Massachusetts
Connecticut
Rhode Island
Pittsburgh Steelers
Heinz Field
Pittsburgh, Pennsylvania
New Jersey
Ohio
Delaware
Maryland
West Virginia
Virginia
Baltimore Ravens
M&T Bank Stadium
Baltimore, Maryland
North Carolina
South Carolina

Torrey Smith cradles a touchdown catch during the Ravens' January 2015 playoff win.

FUN FACT

The NFL created new divisions in 2002. In the 17 years that followed, either the Ravens or Steelers won their division's title 13 times.

On January 3, 2015, the air was getting cooler. Players could see their breath. The Ravens were ready. They had faced the Steelers three times in the playoffs. Baltimore lost all three. The Ravens hoped to turn things around.

It was the third quarter. The Ravens led 13–9. Now they faced third down. Quarterback Joe Flacco **scrambled**. He found some space. Then he found a receiver. Torrey Smith was open in the end zone. Flacco threw a laser from the 17-yard line. Touchdown! The Ravens went on to win 30–17. And the best part? They did it in Pittsburgh.

The Steelers have played at Heinz Field since 2001.

CHAPTER 3

Battle-Tested Bruisers

Only fifty seconds remained. The Ravens were at home. They led the Steelers 9–6. But the Steelers were hungry. A win would give them the 2008 division title.

Ben Roethlisberger looked right. Nothing. The Steelers quarterback ran to the left. Nothing there, either. He went back to the right. There was Santonio Holmes in the end zone. Roethlisberger threw the ball. Holmes caught it. He fell forward out of the end zone. It didn't matter. His toes were still in when he made the catch. The Steelers had won again. The rivalry continued.

FUN FACT

Ben Roethlisberger made his NFL debut in 2004 against the Ravens in a 30–13 loss.

At 6 feet 5 inches and 240 pounds, Ben Roethlisberger (7) is a beast in Pittsburgh's backfield.

Behind linebacker Ray Lewis, the 2000 Ravens gave up just 165 points, an NFL record.

Some of Roethlisberger's best games were against the Ravens. The Ravens never made it easy, though. **Linebacker** Terrell Suggs loved to tackle him. And he was hardly alone. Baltimore became known for its tough defenses. Linebacker Ray Lewis was intense. He made plays all over the field. Defensive tackle Haloti Ngata was a force, too. Ed Reed was awesome, as well. He was a shutdown cornerback.

Pittsburgh's defense was good too, though. James Harrison loved to take down Joe Flacco. Troy Polamalu flew through the air to make tackles. He always seemed to know what the Ravens were going to do.

FUN FACT

From 2000 to 2018, 19 of the 42 games between the Ravens and Steelers were decided by three points or fewer.

Baltimore's M&T Bank Stadium

Pittsburgh had won its final game in 2018. The sky grew dark. Yet the players stayed on the field. Many fans stayed, too. They all stared at the video board. The Ravens were still playing. If Baltimore won, it would go to the playoffs. A loss would send Pittsburgh.

Rookie Lamar Jackson led the Ravens. He had taken over as quarterback. His Ravens led the Cleveland Browns by two points. The Browns had one last shot. C. J. Mosley ended it. He intercepted a pass. The Ravens won. Even when they weren't playing each other, the Ravens and Steelers were rivals.

FUN FACT

The Ravens are named after a poem written by Baltimore resident Edgar Allan Poe. The team's mascot is a raven named Poe.

Quarterback Lamar Jackson ushered in a new era for the Ravens in 2018.

CHAPTER 4

Passionate Ravens fans cheer their team to victory.

Black and Yellow, or Purple?

Don't wear purple the week before the Ravens game. Everyone on the Steelers' staff knows that. One time an employee wore a purple shirt. The team sent her home to change. Pittsburgh is all about black and gold. All three major pro sports teams in town wear those colors.

Terrible Towels are bright yellow. Steelers fans bring them to games. They twirl the towels in the air. Former radio announcer Myron Cope started the tradition. It began during the 1975 playoffs. Cope told fans to bring yellow towels to wave. The Steelers were hosting the Baltimore Colts. And the Steelers won. A tradition was born.

FUN FACT

Terrible Towels have been photographed at the South Pole, the Great Wall of China, and even the International Space Station.

There are older rivalries in the NFL. Not many right now are as strong as the Steelers and Ravens. A lot of it is because both teams are similar. They are often known for their strong defenses. Both teams play hard, too. Players know they will probably have bumps and bruises afterward.

It's worth it for the win, though. Terrell Suggs loved playing the Steelers. He said it was the one game his Ravens better win. Pittsburgh's James Harrison said he hated losing to anybody. But losing to the Ravens was the worst.

BLAME THE TERRIBLE TOWEL?

In 2008, a Ravens wide receiver stomped on the Terrible Towel. The Ravens lost all three games to the Steelers that year. That included the conference title game. The Steelers won the Super Bowl.

The Ravens defense can often shut down even the most powerful offenses.

The Ravens and Steelers both want to win when they play each other. They also respect each other. Ben Roethlisberger told reporters that the players would hit each other hard. Then they'd help them up and tell them nice job. At the end of the game they'd shake hands. They'd say they had fun. And they couldn't wait for the next time they played.

Even after a fierce battle, Steelers quarterback Ben Roethlisberger, right, and Ravens quarterback Joe Flacco shake hands.

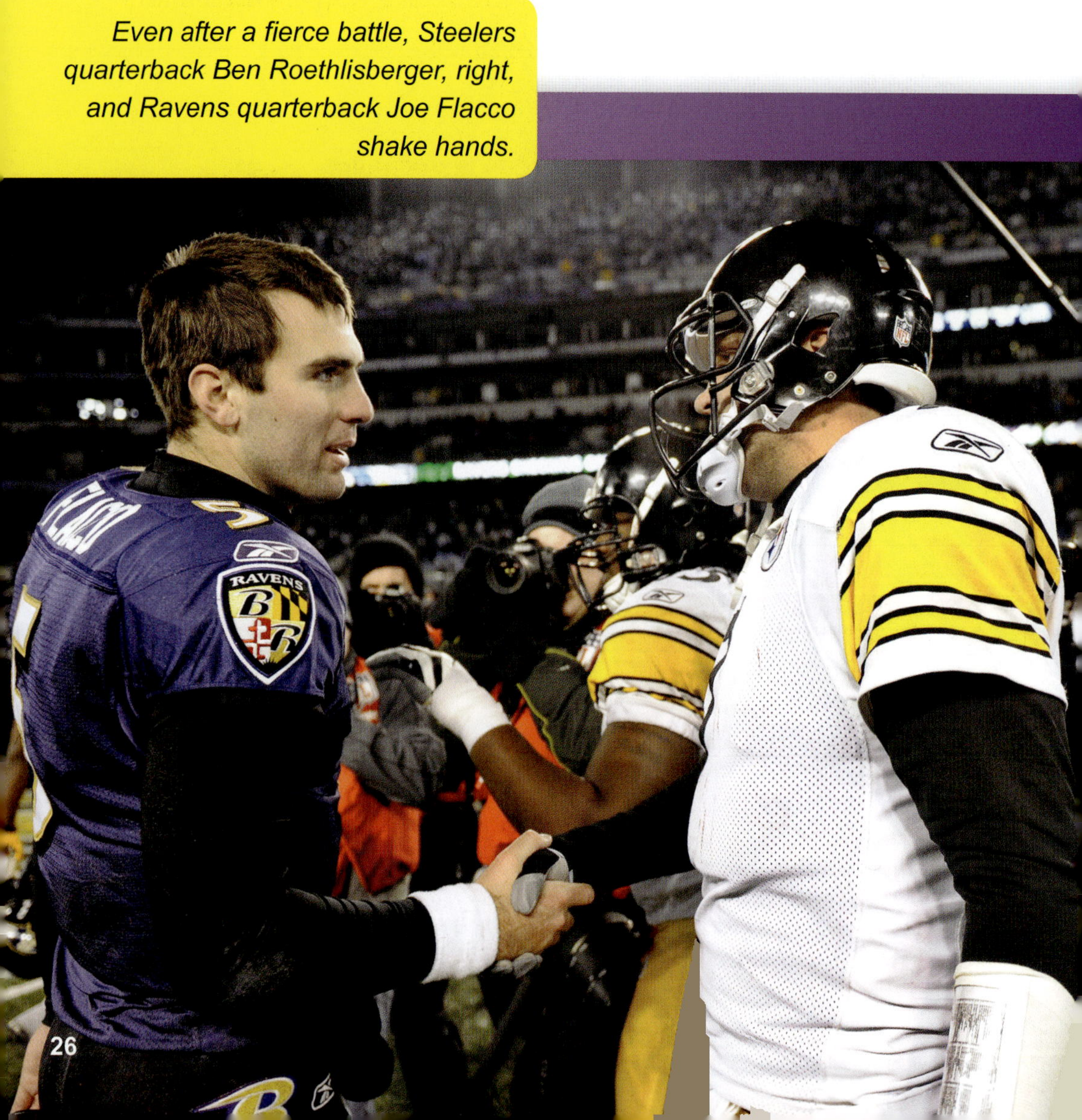

HEAD TO HEAD

STATS

Through the 2018 season

RAVENS		STEELERS
21	WINS	25
45.7	WINNING PERCENTAGE	54.3
903	POINTS SCORED	931
1	PLAYOFF WINS	3
4 (2015-16)	LONGEST WIN STREAK	(1997-99) (2001-03) 5
2	TOTAL SUPER BOWL VICTORIES	6

BEYOND THE BOOK

After reading the book, it's time to think about what you learned. Try the following exercises to jumpstart your ideas.

THINK

THAT'S NEWS TO ME. The conference title game in January 2009 between the Steelers and the Ravens was one of the biggest games of the rivalry. Where can you get more information on this game? What kinds of news sources will you look for? Where will you find them? What information could you learn?

CREATE

PRIMARY SOURCES. Primary sources are first-hand accounts of events. Where could you go to find primary sources of information on the rivalry between the Ravens and the Steelers? Make a list.

SHARE

WHAT'S YOUR OPINION? The book says that some of Ben Roethlisberger's best games were against the Ravens. Do you agree? Find evidence to support your opinion. Think of the places you could go to find statistics. Look for facts in the text. Share your opinion with a classmate. Did you convince him or her?

GROW

REAL-LIFE RESEARCH. You can learn a lot about football from reading. Where could you go to watch a football game? What might you learn by attending a game that you might not learn from reading? Where else can you learn more about the Steelers and the Ravens?

Visit www.ninjaresearcher.com/0844 to learn how to take your research skills and book report writing to the next level!

RESEARCH

SEARCH LIKE A PRO

Learn about how to use search engines to find useful websites.

FACT OR FAKE?

Discover how you can tell a trusted website from an untrustworthy resource.

TEXT DETECTIVE

Explore how to zero in on the information you need most.

SHOW YOUR WORK

Research responsibly—learn how to cite sources.

WRITE

GET TO THE POINT

Learn how to express your main ideas.

PLAN OF ATTACK

Learn prewriting exercises and create an outline.

DOWNLOADABLE REPORT FORMS

Further Resources

BOOKS

Osborne, M. K. *Superstars of the Pittsburgh Steelers.* Amicus, 2019.

Scheff, Matt. *Fierce NFL Rivalries: 12 Super-Charged Matchups.* 12-Story Library, 2016.

Smolka, Bo. *Baltimore Ravens.* Abdo Publishing, 2017.

WEBSITES

Factsurfer.com gives you a safe, fun way to find more information.

1. Go to www.factsurfer.com.
2. Enter “Steelers vs. Ravens” into the search box and click .
3. Select your book cover to see a list of related websites.

Glossary

debut: A debut is someone's first appearance. Ben Roethlisberger made his NFL debut against the Ravens.

division: A division is a group of teams who play each other twice in each NFL season, and the team with the best record from each division automatically qualifies for the playoffs. The Ravens and Steelers are fierce division rivals.

interception: An interception is when a defensive player catches a pass intended for an opponent. Troy Polamalu scored a touchdown after making an interception.

linebacker: A linebacker is a defensive player responsible for stopping the run, covering the pass, and blitzing the quarterback. Linebacker Ray Lewis was a force in the middle of the field.

rookie: A rookie is a player in his first year in the league. Joe Flacco wanted to become the first rookie quarterback to lead his team to the Super Bowl.

safety: A safety is a defensive player responsible for covering passing plays. Troy Polamalu was a reliable safety for the Steelers.

scramble: To scramble is when a quarterback runs with the ball to escape pressure. Joe Flacco scrambled to buy more time.

snap: The snap is when the center starts a play by passing the ball beneath his legs. Joe Flacco took the snap and dropped back to pass.

Index

PHOTO CREDITS

The images in this book are reproduced through the courtesy of: Don Wright/AP Images, front cover (left), p. 14; Peter Read Miller/AP Images, front cover (right); EFKS/Shutterstock Images, front cover (background); Jeff Bukowski/Shutterstock Images, pp. 3 (left), 3 (right); Keith Srakocic/AP Images, pp. 4–5; Julie Jacobson/AP Images, pp. 6–7; Rob Carr/AP Images, pp. 8, 16–17; enterlinedesign/Shutterstock Images, p. 9; Gene J. Puskar/AP Images, p. 11; Red Line Editorial, pp. 13, 27; Robert Pernell/Shutterstock Images, p. 15; Chuck Burton/AP Images, p. 18; Nicole S Glass/Shutterstock Images, p. 19; Library of Congress, p. 20; Carolyn Kaster/AP Images, p. 21; Jamie Lamor Thompson/Shutterstock Images, pp. 22–23; dean bertoncelj/Shutterstock Images, p. 24; Nick Wass/AP Images, pp. 25, 26; Mtsaride/Shutterstock Images, p. 30.

ABOUT THE AUTHOR

Karen Price lives in Pittsburgh with her husband and their two cats. In addition to sports she loves spending time outside, reading, and listening to music.